Animal Workers

Julie Haydon

Chapter 1
Using Animals

For thousands of years, animals have been used to carry people. Animals have been used to carry **goods**, too.

Animals can be used to:

- carry people
- carry or pull heavy objects
- carry messages

Today machines do many of the jobs that animals once did. However animals are still used in some places to carry people and goods.

Chapter 2
Elephants

Elephants are the largest animals on land. They use their long trunks for doing many things, such as smelling, drinking, and lifting objects. Elephants also have huge teeth called tusks. Elephants use their tusks as tools and **weapons**.

Elephants are very smart animals and can be trained to work with people. Elephants can carry people on their backs. They can also carry, push, or pull heavy objects.

5

A Closer Look

These elephants work in the forests of **Thailand**. People cut down the trees for the wood. Then the elephants carry, drag, or push the logs out of the forests. Some logging elephants can drag a load of one and a half tons of logs!

Machines could pull the logs out of the forest. However the machines rip the plants and dig holes in the ground. Elephants' feet are gentle on the forest. They do not rip the plants. They do not make holes in the ground.

Chapter 3
Sled Dogs

There are many different kinds of dogs. Sled dogs are medium-sized, working dogs of mixed **breed**. They are strong and can run quickly. Their thick double coats keep them warm in very cold places. Sled dogs are smart and can follow orders.

Sled dogs are trained to work as a team to pull a sled over snow and ice. It takes many months of training to get the team to pull together. A team of sled dogs can pull a sled and a person for hundreds of miles.

A Closer Look

These people and dogs are at the start of a sled race. Some sled races are short. This race will take many days.

The driver stands on the back of the sled. Sometimes the driver holds onto the sled and runs behind it. The dogs wear special socks called **booties**. The booties help to keep the dogs' paws warm and dry.

booties

Chapter 4
Horses

Horses have large, strong bodies and can run fast. They can take air in quickly through their large **nostrils**. People use horses for work and transportation.

Horses can be trained to pull wagons and other objects. They can be trained to carry people, too. Horses can be ridden with or without a saddle.

A Closer Look

These horses are carrying police officers. The horses help the police officers do their work. The police officers sit up high. This makes it easier for them to watch the crowd.

The police officers and the horses can move quickly when needed. They can go places where it is hard for vehicles to go.

Chapter 5

Homing Pigeons

Homing pigeons are different from the pigeons found in parks or on city sidewalks. They are trained to find their way home from hundreds of miles away. Some homing pigeons can fly at speeds up to 60 miles per hour. They do not need to stop for food or rest during these long flights.

Some homing pigeons are trained to carry small objects.
They have been used during wars to carry messages,
cameras, film, and maps. This pigeon is carrying a
message in a tiny case on its leg.

A Closer Look

These people are in a **raft** on a river. They are having fun. Some photographs are taken. The film is put inside a small backpack. The backpack is put onto a trained homing pigeon. The pigeon is set free. It flies home.

There is a photo shop at its home. Workers in the shop **develop** the film. When the people finish rafting, they pick up their photographs.

Chapter 6
Camels

For thousands of years, camels have been used to transport people and goods through the desert. These animals can live in very hot places. They can go without food and water for many days. Camels have one or two humps on their backs that have fat, not water, in them.

Camels are strong animals with powerful legs. They are trained to pull **plows** and turn waterwheels. Camels can travel where vehicles cannot go. Sometimes they are ridden in races.

A Closer Look

These camels are carrying heavy loads. The people who own the camels move from place to place. The camels carry everything that the people own.

Some of the time, the people and their camels travel over sand. Camels have two large toes on each foot. These toes are wide and padded. They help the camel walk over soft sand.

Glossary

booties   special socks that sled dogs wear to keep their paws warm and dry

breed   a group of animals that look similar and have the same family line

develop   turn film into photographs

goods   things people own

nostrils   the two openings in the nose

plows   farm equipment used for turning up the soil before planting seeds

raft   an open, rubber boat that can be moved with paddles

Thailand   a country in southeast Asia

weapons   objects used for fighting

Index